OCEANS ALIVE

Orcas

by Anne Wendorff

BELLWETHER MEDIA · MINNEAPOLIS, MN

Note to Librarians, Teachers, and Parents:

Blastoff! Readers are carefully developed by literacy experts and combine standards-based content with developmentally appropriate text.

Level 1 provides the most support through repetition of high-frequency words, light text, predictable sentence patterns, and strong visual support.

Level 2 offers early readers a bit more challenge through varied simple sentences, increased text load, and less repetition of high-frequency words.

Level 3 advances early-fluent readers toward fluency through increased text and concept load, less reliance on visuals, longer sentences, and more literary language.

Level 4 builds reading stamina by providing more text per page, increased use of punctuation, greater variation in sentence patterns, and increasingly challenging vocabulary.

Level 5 encourages children to move from "learning to read" to "reading to learn" by providing even more text, varied writing styles, and less familiar topics.

Whichever book is right for your reader, Blastoff! Readers are the perfect books to build confidence and encourage a love of reading that will last a lifetime!

This edition first published in 2009 by Bellwether Media.

No part of this publication may be reproduced in whole or in part without written permission of the publisher. For information regarding permission, write to Bellwether Media Inc., Attention: Permissions Department, Post Office Box 19349, Minneapolis, MN 55419.

Library of Congress Cataloging-in-Publication Data
Wendorff, Anne.
  Orcas / by Anne Wendorff.
    p. cm. – (Blastoff! readers. Oceans alive)
  Summary: "Simple text and full color photographs introduce beginning readers to orcas. Developed by literacy experts for students in kindergarten through third grade"–Provided by publisher.
  Includes bibliographical references and index.
  ISBN-13: 978-1-60014-205-5 (hardcover : alk. paper)
  ISBN-10: 1-60014-205-2 (hardcover : alk. paper)
  1. Killer whale–Juvenile literature. 2. Toothed whales–Juvenile literature. I. Title.

QL737.C432W46 2009
599.53'6–dc22   2008017346

Contents

What Is an Orca?	4
What Do Orcas Look Like?	6
Orcas Breaching	10
Hunting with Orcas	14
Orca Pods	18
Glossary	22
To Learn More	23
Index	24

Orcas are **toothed whales**. They live in every ocean on Earth.

They are sometimes
called killer whales.

Orcas are black and white. They are mostly black on top and white on the bottom.

Ocean water can be very cold.
Orcas have a layer of **blubber**
that keeps them warm.

Orcas have big tails to push them through the water.

dorsal fin

They have **dorsal fins** on their backs. Dorsal fins help orcas swim straight.

Orcas **breach** the surface
to breathe.

They breathe through a **blowhole** on the top of their head.

Orcas can breach in different ways.
They can swim to the surface then
dive back under the water.

They can also leap out of the water and fall back in with a splash.

Orcas are good hunters.

They hunt fish, seals,
stingrays, and other
ocean animals.

Orcas have sharp teeth to catch and tear food.

They are also fast swimmers.
This helps them catch food.

Orcas live in groups
called **pods**.

Members of a pod speak
to each other with clicks
and whistles.

Orcas in a pod recognize each other's voices.

Orcas often spend their whole lives together with the same pod.

Glossary

blowhole—a small hole on the top of an orca's head; orcas breathe air through their blowhole.

blubber—a thick layer of fat under the skin; blubber helps keep orcas warm in cold water.

breach—to rise out of the water; orcas breach to breathe air.

dorsal fin—a fin on an orca's back; dorsal fins help orcas swim straight.

pod—a group of orcas that live together; between 6 and 40 orcas live in a pod.

toothed whale—a whale with teeth for catching and tearing food

To Learn More

AT THE LIBRARY

Herriges, Ann. *Whales*. Minneapolis, Minn.: Bellwether, 2007.

Markle, Sandra. *Killer Whales*. Minneapolis, Minn.: First Avenue Editions, 2004.

Simon, Seymour. *Killer Whales*. San Francisco, Calif.: Chronicle Books, 2002.

ON THE WEB
Learning more about orcas is as easy as 1, 2, 3.

1. Go to www.factsurfer.com

2. Enter "orcas" into search box.

3. Click the "Surf" button and you will see a list of related web sites.

With factsurfer.com, finding more information is just a click away.

Index

animals, 15

blowhole, 11

blubber, 7

breaching, 10, 12

breathing, 10, 11

clicks, 19

dorsal fins, 9

Earth, 4

fish, 15

food, 16, 17

hunting, 14, 15

oceans, 4

pods, 18, 19, 20, 21

seals, 15

speaking, 19

tails, 8

teeth, 16

toothed whales, 4

voices, 20

whistles, 19

The images in this book are reproduced through the courtesy of: Jamie Garrison, front cover; Juniors Bildarchiv / agefotostock, pp. 4-5, 6, 16; Steven J. Kazlowski / Alamy, p. 7; Thomas Szymanski, p. 8; Flip Nicklin / Getty Images, p. 9; J. A. Kraulis / Masterfile, pp. 10-11; ARCO/P. Wegner / agefotostock, pp. 12-13; Jeff Foott / Getty Images, pp. 14-15, 15 (inset); Rolf Hicker / agefotostock, p. 17; Evgeniya Lazareva, pp. 18-19; Norbert We / Getty Images, pp. 20-21.